# Health, Illness, and Death
# IN THE TIME OF COVID-19

Bradley Steffens

ReferencePoint
Press

San Diego, CA

## About the Author

Bradley Steffens is a novelist, a poet, and an award-winning author of more than sixty nonfiction books for children and young adults.

Picture Credits:

Cover: Tempura/iStock
8: kool99/iStock
12: Kateryna Kon/iStock
15: Juanmonino/iStock
18: Semnic/Shutterstock.com
21: CDC/Science Source
28: Scott S. Hamrick/KRT/Newscom

31: Olga Miltsova/Shutterstock.com
34: Associated Press
38: Drazen Zigic/Shutterstock.com
44: zstock/Shutterstock.com
48: RolandL
53: Associated Press
55: Dmitriy Kandinskiy/Shutterstock.com

LIBRARY OF CONGRESS CATALOGING-IN-PUBLICATION DATA

Names: Steffens, Bradley, 1955- author.
Title: Health, illness, and death in the time of COVID-19 / by Bradley Steffens.
Description: San Diego, CA : ReferencePoint Press, 2021. | Series: Understanding the COVID-19 pandemic | Includes bibliographical references and index.
Identifiers: LCCN 2020045627 (print) | LCCN 2020045628 (ebook) | ISBN 9781678200343 (library binding) | ISBN 9781678200350 (ebook)
Subjects: LCSH: COVID-19 (Disease)--Juvenile literature. | COVID-19 (Disease)--Economic aspects--Juvenile literature. | COVID-19 (Disease)--Government policy--Juvenile literature. | COVID-19 (Disease)--Social aspects--Juvenile literature. | COVID-19 (Disease)--Prevention--Juvenile literature. | Epidemics--Juvenile literature.
Classification: LCC RA644.C67 S72 2021 (print) | LCC RA644.C67 (ebook) | DDC 362.1962/414--dc23
LC record available at https://lccn.loc.gov/2020045627
LC ebook record available at https://lccn.loc.gov/2020045628

# CONTENTS

# The COVID-19 Pandemic:
## The First Nine Months of 2020

### January

(11) China reports first known death from mysterious virus that infected dozens in Wuhan in December.

(20) WHO reports that Japan, South Korea, and Thailand have first confirmed virus cases outside of mainland China.

(30) WHO declares global health emergency.

(31) US restricts travel from China.

### February

(2) Philippines reports first coronavirus death outside of China.

(5) Japan quarantines *Diamond Princess* cruise ship; within 2 weeks the ship has more than 600 infections.

(11) WHO names the disease caused by the new coronavirus COVID-19 (for *coronavirus disease 2019*).

(23) Europe's first major outbreak occurs in Italy.

(26) Brazil has Latin America's first known case of coronavirus.

### March

(13) US president Donald Trump officially declares national emergency.

(19) California becomes first US state to enact statewide shutdown.

(24) Officials announce 1-year postponement of 2020 Tokyo Summer Olympics.

(26) US becomes world leader in confirmed coronavirus infections.

(27) President Trump signs $2 trillion economic stimulus bill sent to him by Congress.

### April

(2) Pandemic shutdowns have cost nearly 10 million Americans their jobs.

(10) Coronavirus cases surge in Russia.

(14) IMF warns of worst global downturn since Great Depression.

(17) President Trump encourages protests of social distancing restrictions.

(26) Pandemic has killed more than 200,000 and sickened more than 2.8 million worldwide.

(30) Several major airlines begin requiring face masks.

**May**

1. FDA authorizes remdesivir as an emergency treatment for COVID-19.

17. Japan and Germany fall into recession.

26. Widespread protests begin after George Floyd is killed by Minneapolis police; because many protesters wear masks, feared virus outbreaks do not occur.

27. US has more than 100,000 COVID-19 deaths, surpassing all other nations.

**June**

4. Previously spared regions of Middle East, Latin America, Africa, and South Asia have large spikes.

11. Coronavirus cases in Africa exceed 200,000, with one-fourth in South Africa.

20. Florida and South Carolina are among 19 US states experiencing sharp rise in new infections.

28. Final phase of clinical trials for AstraZeneca–University of Oxford COVID-19 vaccine begins in Brazil.

**July**

11. For the first time, President Trump wears a mask during a public appearance.

16. Georgia's governor rescinds local government mask mandates.

17. After easing restrictions in May, skyrocketing infections force India to reimpose lockdown.

27. Final phase of clinical trials for Moderna COVID-19 vaccine begins in the US.

**August**

9. New Zealand achieves 100 days without a new diagnosis of coronavirus.

11. Amid global skepticism, Russia announces first approved-for-use coronavirus vaccine.

17. Democrats begin first-ever, all-virtual convention to nominate the party's presidential candidate, Joe Biden.

23. FDA authorizes convalescent plasma as an emergency treatment for COVID-19.

27. Before a crowd of about 1,500 people, President Trump accepts Republican presidential nomination.

**September**

8. Nine of the leading drug companies developing COVID-19 vaccines pledge in writing to put safety before speed.

21. President Trump tells supporters at an Ohio rally that COVID "affects virtually nobody."

30. The pandemic has killed more than 1 million people and sickened nearly 34 million worldwide. In the US, the pandemic has killed nearly 207,000 people and sickened more than 7 million. Two days later, on October 2, President Trump tweets that he and First Lady Melania Trump have tested positive for the virus that causes COVID-19.

Based on Derrick Bryson Taylor, "A Timeline of the Coronavirus Pandemic," *New York Times*, July 21, 2020. www.nytimes.com.

# Mass Killer

Experts had warned the world for decades. "The single biggest threat to man's continued dominance on the planet is the virus,"[1] wrote Nobel laureate Joshua Lederberg in a 1988 article entitled "Medical Science, Infectious Disease, and the Unity of Humankind." The eye-opening quote was featured at the beginning of the 1991 medical thriller *The Hot Zone* by Richard Preston. Even earlier, in 1985, virologist Edwin Kilbourne had brainstormed a worst-case virus scenario, dubbing his imaginary pathogen the "maximally malignant (mutant) virus," or MMMV. "For maximal transmissibility," wrote Kilbourne, "MMMV, like influenza virus, should replicate in the lower respiratory tract [lungs]"[2] and be transmitted through the air by coughing and sneezing. It would have a long latency period—the period between becoming contagious and the onset of symptoms—so people could spread it before they knew they had it. And it would have the ability to survive outside the body, living on countertops and other surfaces where people could touch it and introduce it into their bodies and circulating through the air in rooms, airplanes, and buses. Such a virus could kill millions.

## The World Was Unprepared

Despite the warnings of Lederberg, Preston, Kilbourne, and others, the world was not prepared to respond to such a virulent, deadly pathogen when one finally appeared. On December 31, 2019, the Wuhan Municipal Health Commission in Wuhan, China, reported a cluster of unusual suspected pneumonia cases to the World Health Organization (WHO). One week later Chinese authorities identified a new, or novel, coronavirus as the cause of these illnesses. Like Kilbourne's nightmarish virus, the novel coronavirus had a long latency period, replicated deep in the lungs, could live outside the body, and could be transmitted through the air. On February 11, 2020, the WHO named the new disease caused by this virus COVID-19 (for *coronavirus disease 2019*). By the time the WHO declared a global public health emergency on January 30, 2020, Chinese New Year celebrants—both domestic and foreign—were streaming home, carrying the killer virus with them. The WHO's January 30 situation report stated that there were 7,818 confirmed cases worldwide, with 82 cases reported in eighteen countries outside China.

> "The single biggest threat to man's continued dominance on the planet is the virus."[1]
>
> —Joshua Lederberg, a molecular biologist and recipient of the Nobel Prize in Physiology or Medicine

Without a blueprint to follow for curbing a pandemic, the nations of the world were left to come up with their own plans of action. What followed was an array of disease mitigation efforts, some proven but others completely untested. Qatar was the first country to order a lockdown, restricting the movement of foreign workers in its industrial zone on March 11, 2020. The next day Ireland closed schools and colleges and banned indoor gatherings of more than one hundred people and outdoor gatherings of more than five hundred. Other countries issued lockdowns of their own. Sweden adopted a different strategy. Its government chose to keep schools and businesses open and let the disease run its course. In the United States the decisions about school closings, lockdowns, face coverings, social distancing, and testing were left to individual states and, in some states, to individual cities. Shortages of personal protective equipment put frontline workers in peril, leading to infection and death rates from COVID-19 that were ten times higher than the rates for the general population.

Kits to test for the disease were not broadly available for months, leaving authorities in the dark about where the disease was and how many people actually had it. Work began on finding a vaccine, but vaccine development (which includes testing for safety and effectiveness) takes months, if not years.

## Life Upended

By September 30, 2020, the pandemic had sickened nearly 34 million people worldwide and killed more than 1 million. In the United States, which had more infections and more deaths than any other nation, as of that same date the pandemic had sickened more than 7 million people and killed nearly 207,000. The COVID-19 fatality rate—the percentage of people with the disease who died from it—stands at 3 percent. The rate is low among young patients but rises dramatically with age to 15 percent in patients eighty years old and older. Underlying health conditions—including obesity, diabetes, cardiovascular disease, and respiratory disease—increase the risk of severe illness and death. About 40 percent of people with COVID-19 experience mild disease. Another 40 percent experience moderate disease, including pneumonia. About 15 percent of cases are classified as severe, and 5 percent are critical.

The COVID-19 pandemic has upended life in the United States, triggering the worst recession in decades, the highest unemployment since the Great Depression, and the postponement or cancellation of many public events—from Broadway plays to the Tokyo Summer Olympics. Students and teachers have been hit hard, with irreplaceable learning opportunities and extracurricular activities simply scrubbed from the academic calendar. Some states, like Florida, reopened early. Others, like California, remained locked down for a long time. Many people believe that only a safe and effective vaccine will return life to normal. But as the experts have warned, normal will not last forever. Perhaps the one benefit of this pandemic will be that the world is better prepared for the next one.

# CHAPTER ONE

# How COVID-19 Kills

Chantee Mack understood the dangers of COVID-19. A disease intervention specialist for Prince George's County in Maryland, Mack had worked for years with people who had life-threatening diseases. The more Mack learned about COVID-19, the more she realized that this new disease was especially dangerous for people with preexisting health conditions, including heart disease, diabetes, asthma, and obesity. Obese herself, she counted herself among those most at risk.

## Exposure and Illness

When the COVID-19 pandemic hit Prince George's County in March 2020, the county government told four hundred of its five hundred public health care workers to stay home, but Mack, forty-four, was not among them. She was considered "essential" and required to report to work. Since she performed most of her duties by phone and on a computer, Mack applied to work from home during the pandemic. Her immediate supervisors supported her requests, but upper management denied them.

Mack was not working on the front lines of the county's COVID-19 response, but this did not mean she was safe. On March 19, 2020, the same day that Maryland governor Larry Hogan announced a ban on gatherings of more than ten people, Mack attended a staff meeting where more than twenty people sat next to each other in a U shape around the room. One of those in attendance, Candace Young, felt ill the next day. A few days later, Young tested positive for COVID-19. Nine of the nineteen people who worked with Young—including some who attended the meeting—soon also tested positive. Mack was one of them.

As Mack had feared, the disease hit her hard. She was one of four coworkers who were hospitalized with COVID-19. The doctors placed her on a ventilator to help with her breathing and later ordered a blood transfusion to strengthen her immune system. For four long weeks, Mack fought hard for her life. "She was a good soul—strong," says her brother Roland Mack. In May, Mack's kidneys failed, and she developed bleeding in the brain. On May 11, 2020, her heart stopped. The woman who had spent her life helping others fight diseases had succumbed to her own. "Just not having my sister around no more, it's going to be a tough one," says Roland. "I feel alone now that she's gone."[3]

> "She was a good soul—strong. Just not having my sister around no more, it's going to be a tough one. I feel alone now that she's gone."[3]
>
> —Roland Mack, the brother of COVID-19 victim Chantee Mack

## A New Virus

Mack's life was unique, but her death followed a pattern that has become chillingly familiar. By late October 2020, according to the Johns Hopkins Coronavirus Resource Center, more than 225,000 Americans had perished from COVID-19. Mack was likely infected when she inhaled an airborne droplet, known as an aerosol, containing the COVID-19 coronavirus. This probably occurred in the meeting at work, but it could have happened anytime she was near to or in an enclosed place with a carrier of the disease.

The coronavirus gets its name from the crown-like structure, or corona, of spikes that cover its surface. The spikes of the crown allow the virus to bind to a protein on the surface of some human cells. This protein is known as ACE2. Normally, ACE2 helps

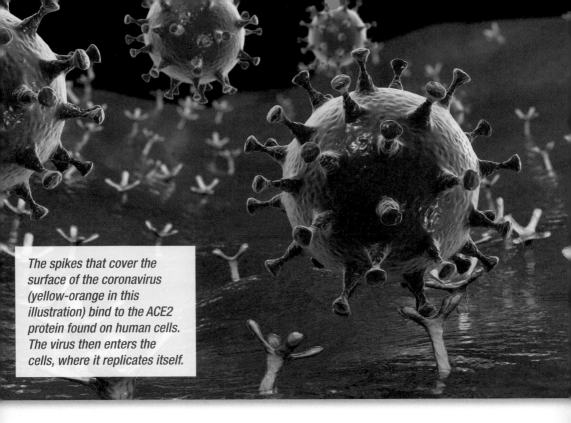

The spikes that cover the surface of the coronavirus (yellow-orange in this illustration) bind to the ACE2 protein found on human cells. The virus then enters the cells, where it replicates itself.

regulate blood pressure in the body. However, the spikes on the coronavirus fit into its structure like a key into a lock. This enables the virus to bind to the cell and enter it. Once inside the cell, the virus uses the cell's replicating processes to make copies of itself. These new viruses move through the body, attaching themselves to ACE2 receptors, entering cells, and making more copies of themselves.

## First Symptoms

Once inside the body, the virus invades the cells of the upper respiratory system. The immune system recognizes the virus as a pathogen—a microorganism that can cause disease. The body unleashes disease-fighting proteins, known as antibodies, to attack the invaders. It also releases T cells to destroy cells already infected with the virus.

The body's reaction, known as an immune response, causes many of the symptoms associated with COVID-19. This includes a rise in body temperature, resulting in a high fever—a hallmark of the disease. Many COVID-19 victims also develop headaches, body aches, a dry cough, sore throat, and a loss of taste and smell. The immune response can also cause blood vessels to dilate so they can rush antibodies throughout the body. The dilation of blood vessels can cause organs to become inflamed, disrupting their function. This can lead to kidney failure, as happened in Mack's case.

The immune response of some people is able to stop the virus in the upper respiratory system. Some of these people may not experience any symptoms. They are known as asymptomatic. However, they are still contagious. They can spread the disease by shedding large amounts of the virus by speaking, coughing, or sneezing.

## Sisters Who Were Close in Life and in Death

Corrina and Cheryl Thinn, both members of the Navajo Nation, were extremely close. The sisters lived together with their mother, helped out with each other's children, and even worked at adjacent desks at Tuba City Regional Health Care in northern Arizona. Corrina, age forty-four, was a social worker. Cheryl, age forty, reviewed patient care. In March 2020, without any protective equipment, Corrina met with a patient who was showing symptoms of COVID-19. The patient died from the disease a couple of days later, and Corrina became ill as well. She worried about having infected Cheryl, who had rheumatoid arthritis, a condition that worsens the effects of COVID-19.

Corrina's worst fears were soon realized. Cheryl came down with the disease, and it hit her hard. She was admitted to the Tuba City hospital. Corrina also got worse and went to the emergency room at the same hospital, although Cheryl never knew it. Cheryl died on April 11; Corrina died eighteen days later—two of the hundreds of health care workers who have died from COVID-19. They also were among the hundreds of deaths among the Navajo Nation, the group with the highest per capita infection rate in the United States.

# Infecting the Lungs

If the body does not stop the coronavirus in the upper respiratory system, it can make its way down the windpipe and into the lungs. Normally, air that is taken into the lung travels through its branches and makes its way to small air sacs known as alveoli. The oxygen in the inhaled air passes through the alveoli and enters into the bloodstream, where it is carried to the heart and then pumped throughout the body. However, the alveoli are lined with cells that are coated with ACE2 proteins, making them vulnerable to the coronavirus.

If the virus infects the lungs, the immune system releases even more antibodies to attack it. These antibodies are suspended in a fluid that seeps out of the blood vessels. This fluid can collect in the alveoli, blocking the passageways through which oxygen enters the blood. At the same time, the T cells can kill cells that are infected with the virus. The dead cells mix with the fluid already in the alveoli, further obstructing the oxygen passageways—a condition known as pneumonia. The fluid reduces the amount of oxygen entering the bloodstream, causing shortness of breath—the feeling that a person needs more air. Short, shallow breathing is one of the most serious symptoms of COVID-19. A person with this condition often coughs in an attempt to clear the lungs and get more air.

The lack of oxygen in the bloodstream can set off a chain reaction that damages organs. One of the dangers of COVID-19 is that people feel sick but wait before seeking treatment. By then, their blood oxygen levels can be very low, and their organs may already be damaged. Shortness of breath is a symptom of COVID-19 that requires immediate treatment. Typically, doctors put these patients on a ventilator, which pumps air with extra oxygen through a tube, down the throat, and into the lungs.

For some patients, receiving the added oxygen from a ventilator or another breathing device is all they need to recover, but that has not been the case for hundreds of thousands of people. In many instances the witch's brew of extra fluid, dead cells, and mucus can fill a large number of the alveoli, causing a condition known as acute respiratory distress syndrome (ARDS). Patients with ARDS are unable to get enough oxygen in their systems to support their organs, resulting in death.

In addition to causing the lungs to fill with fluid, COVID-19 can also cause blood clots to form in the lining of the lungs. Like the excess fluid, these tiny clots prevent oxygen from entering the bloodstream, starving the organs of oxygen and contributing to death. The inability to get enough oxygen into the blood, known as respiratory failure, is one of the most common causes of COVID-19 deaths. "[The disease] can attack almost anything in the body with devastating consequences," says Harlan Krumholz, a cardiologist at Yale New Haven Hospital. "Its ferocity is breathtaking and humbling."[4]

"[COVID-19] can attack almost anything in the body with devastating consequences. Its ferocity is breathtaking and humbling."[4]

—Harlan Krumholz, a cardiologist at Yale New Haven Hospital

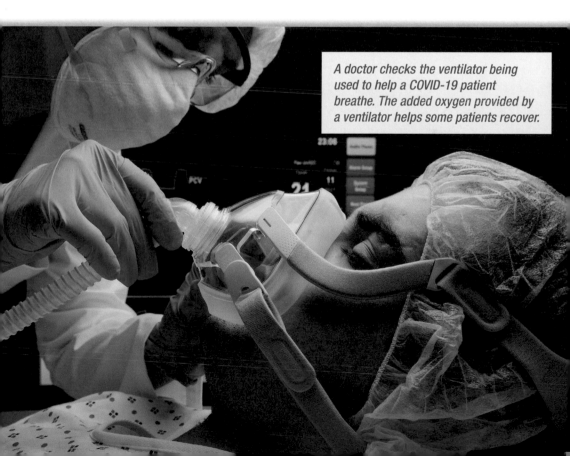

A doctor checks the ventilator being used to help a COVID-19 patient breathe. The added oxygen provided by a ventilator helps some patients recover.

## Attacking Other Organs

The coronavirus can also attack the kidneys directly. Like the lungs, the kidneys are rich in ACE2 receptors, making them inviting targets for the coronavirus's spiky proteins. The American Society of Nephrology COVID-19 Response Team reports that 10 to 50 percent of COVID-19 patients placed in intensive care units have experienced kidney failure. This finding is in line with earlier studies. A study in Wuhan, China, found that 27 percent of hospitalized patients experienced kidney failure. Mount Sinai Hospital in New York City reports that 46 percent of COVID-19 patients admitted since the beginning of the pandemic have had some kind of kidney damage, and 17 percent required intervention with dialysis machines. These machines perform the kidney's job of removing waste products from a patient's blood.

What medical professionals have found surprising is that only 18 percent of COVID-19 patients with acute kidney injury had a history of kidney problems. In the vast majority of cases—82 percent—COVID-19 itself caused the kidney damage. "The lung is the primary battle zone. But a fraction of the virus possibly at-

## The Coronavirus Family

Scientists first identified the human coronavirus in 1965. Since then scientists have identified six more human coronaviruses. Four, including the first one, cause the common cold, but the other three are deadly. One, known as SARS, was discovered in 2002. It first arose in China and then spread through twenty-eight other countries, infecting more than 8,000 people and killing 774. Another, known as MERS, emerged in 2012. It was first identified in Saudi Arabia and then spread to other parts of the Middle East and among travelers to the region. It resulted in 2,500 cases of infection and 858 deaths. As of September 30, 2020, the coronavirus that causes COVID-19 had infected nearly 34 million people worldwide and caused more than 1 million deaths.

tacks the kidney," says Hongbo Jia, a neuroscientist at the Suzhou Institute of Biomedical Engineering and Technology of the Chinese Academy of Sciences. "And as on the real battlefield, if two places are being attacked at the same time, each place gets worse."[5]

There is mounting evidence that COVID-19 can attack the brain and nervous system as well. In April 2020 scientists in Japan detected traces of the coronavirus in the clear fluid found in the brain and spinal cord of a COVID-19 patient. This patient had developed a swelling of the brain and spinal cord. From 5 to 10 percent of the thousands of COVID-19 patients treated at NYU Langone Medical Center have shown symptoms of brain and nervous system damage, including seizures, loss of consciousness, and loss of smell.

## The Body Turns on Itself

Not everyone responds the same way to COVID-19. About 3 percent of those who test positive for COVID-19 die from it. The other 97 percent recover. Among those who die from the disease are people whose immune system unleashes too many antibodies in an attempt to rid the body of the virus. This overreaction of the immune system is known as a cytokine storm.

Cytokines are signaling molecules that control an immune response. In a cytokine storm, however, the number of cytokines increase far beyond the number needed to fight the infection. As a result, the cytokines direct the immune cells to attack not just the invaders but also healthy cells. This can create more problems than the infection itself. For example, if the immune cells attack the walls of blood vessels, the vessels can begin to leak, causing blood pressure to drop. The leaked blood can form clots that travel through the body, damaging organs. It is possible that the body's own immune system causes brain swelling as immune cells attack healthy tissue during a cytokine storm.

Cytokine storms tend to occur in older patients, who have been exposed to many viruses and bacteria over the course of their lives. Children, who have had less contact with viruses, will fight the disease with a more measured response. "That's the innate immune system," says Alvaro Moreira, a neonatologist at the University of Texas Health Science Center in San Antonio. "We know children are less likely to mount an exaggerated innate response."[6] This is one reason the survival rate of young people is much higher than it is for older people. Children also might be

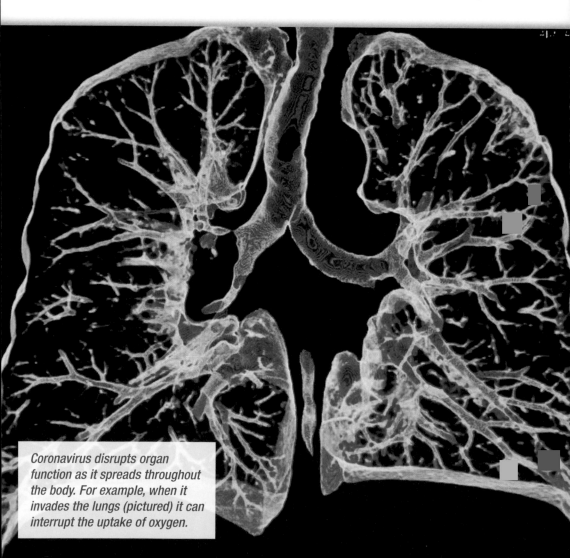

*Coronavirus disrupts organ function as it spreads throughout the body. For example, when it invades the lungs (pictured) it can interrupt the uptake of oxygen.*

spared the severe effects of COVID-19 because they have fewer of the ACE2 receptors on cells in their lungs than adults do. As a result, the virus is confined to their nose and upper respiratory system and does not take hold in their lungs. Consequently, they do not suffer from the lack of oxygen that is so dangerous.

The lack of blood oxygen also stresses the heart, which beats faster and pumps more blood in the attempt to get more oxygen to the rest of the body. Obesity also stresses the heart, which has to work extra hard to pump blood through the larger body. Because of the extra work it has to do, the heart muscle of an obese person becomes thicker, making it more difficult to contract and relax as the heart beats—a characteristic of heart disease.

Because ACE2 performs many functions in the body and can be found on the surface of cells in different organs, the coronavirus can attach itself to cells throughout the body, causing damage in several places at once. It can invade lung tissue, choking off the uptake of oxygen. It can attach to the cells lining the blood vessels, causing blood clots, heart attacks, and cardiac inflammation. It can attack and damage the kidneys, the liver, and the intestines. It can even find its way to the brain, where it causes brain tissue to swell, causes strokes, and impairs brain function. With so many ways to damage the body, COVID-19 is able to prey on people with many different preexisting conditions, making them seriously ill and sometimes causing their death.

# CHAPTER TWO

# How COVID-19 Spreads

In late June 2020 Henry Calderon, a construction worker in San Rafael, California, called his wife, Crisalia, from the emergency room of a nearby hospital. Fighting back tears, Henry told his wife that he had tested positive for COVID-19. He did not have to be hospitalized, but he was worried about infecting Crisalia and the eight other members of their household: their three children, Crisalia's sister, and four other members of her family. "He didn't want to come home," Crisalia remembers. "But what could we do? Where could he go?"[7] With no other options and unsure about the severity of the disease, Henry returned to the crowded apartment. He tried to isolate himself by sleeping in the top bunk of his children's bed, but his strategy did not work. Within a week, eight of the ten people who lived in the apartment tested positive for COVID-19. Fortunately, all members of the family recovered from the virus.

The experience of the Calderons reveals several things that scientists have learned about how COVID-19 spreads. First, because Henry's symptoms were mild, he was not a candidate for hospitalization. Like many others in this position, he did the only thing he could do: he tried to quarantine himself at home. But quarantining is difficult with a large family living in a small apartment. This is how the disease often spreads among family members.

In other instances people who test positive and experience only mild symptoms sometimes ignore the serious risk of spreading the virus and make little effort to self-quarantine. By their actions—or inaction—they often end up passing the virus along to others. "Because, for many, the symptoms [of COVID-19] resemble a mild cold, there is a tendency for the public and politicians to take it less seriously,"[8] writes Nicholas Christakis, a physician and sociologist at Yale University.

## Airborne Transmission

Another thing that helps COVID-19 spread is that it can be passed from person to person without direct physical contact. Viruses can be present in various bodily fluids, including blood, saliva, and mucus. Sometimes the disease is spread by touching something or someone where the virus is present and then touching a membrane that allows the virus to enter the body— the nose, mouth, or eyes. Some viruses can live in droplets of saliva or mucus that are expelled from the body by coughing or sneezing. If another person touches or inhales these droplets, they can become infected.

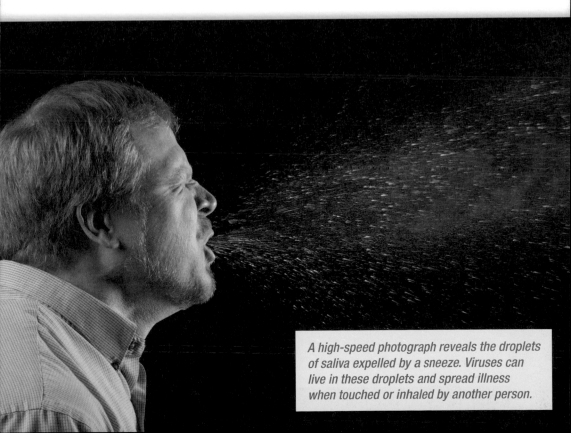

*A high-speed photograph reveals the droplets of saliva expelled by a sneeze. Viruses can live in these droplets and spread illness when touched or inhaled by another person.*

Viruses spread by coughing and sneezing can be easier to control because they are only spread when a person has symptoms of a cold or the flu. The new coronavirus can be spread in these ways, but it can also live in microscopic floating particles known as aerosols. Virus-laden aerosols can be released from a body by exhaling deeply, speaking loudly, or even singing. The person spreading the virus in this way might not have symptoms of the disease. This makes controlling the virus extremely difficult.

The ease with which COVID-19 can be spread became frighteningly clear in Washington State in the spring of 2020 after members of the Skagit Valley Chorale met for a rehearsal on March 10. When they met, there were no known COVID-19 cases in Skagit Valley, and the county health department had not called for closures of public meetings or events. The health department did recommend that people age sixty and above avoid large public

## A Hidden Danger

One of the reasons COVID-19 spreads so quickly is that people who are infected with the virus might not know it for several days. This is because COVID-19 has a long incubation period—the time between becoming infected with a disease and experiencing its symptoms. For COVID-19 the incubation period is two to fourteen days, with an average of six to seven days. By comparison, the incubation for SARS is just two to seven days. As a result, people who have SARS know it within a week and probably sooner, and they can isolate themselves to avoid giving the disease to others. A person with COVID-19 might not know it for up to two weeks.

People can spread a disease during a time known as the latent period. For COVID-19 the latent period is two to four days before the onset of symptoms. Scientists believe that a person with COVID-19 is most contagious in the two days before symptoms appear. People who are infected but still in the latent period will not show outward symptoms, but they can shed the virus through sneezing, coughing, or touching their mouth or nose with their hands.

gatherings. The director of the choir sent members an email asking them not to attend if they felt sick or were showing any symptoms of COVID-19. Many stayed away, but 61 of the choir's 122 members attended. Aware of the pandemic, the members avoided giving each other their customary hugs and handshakes. None of the attendees were sneezing, coughing, or showing any signs of illness. Everyone left the rehearsal feeling fine, but the next day some attendees began to feel ill. Between March 11 and March 15, fifty-three of the sixty-one people who attended the event became ill, with thirty-three confirmed positive for COVID-19. Two of those infected later died.

Researchers later found out that one choir member had cold-like symptoms three days before the rehearsal. That person later tested positive for COVID-19. The researchers concluded that this person, known as the "index case," spread the virus not by touching other choir members but through the air. "An infected choir member spread the virus simply by singing, an activity that forces large amounts of air out of the lungs,"[9] write the scientists. This is similar to what happened in the Calderon family. Although Henry kept his distance from other people, he spread the virus through the air to others in the apartment.

## A Special Danger for People of Color

The Calderons' story also reflects a trend that epidemiologists—scientists who track the spread of diseases through populations—have observed about COVID-19. Namely, Native Americans, Latinos, Blacks, and other people of color have experienced a disproportionate number of COVID-19 illnesses and deaths. The Calderons are Latino. Although Latinos make up only 16 percent of the population in Marin County, the Northern California county where the Calderons live, they account for 75 percent of that county's COVID-19 cases. Nationally, Latinos have 2.8 as many cases of infection as non-Latino Whites, 4.6 as many hospitalizations, and 1.1 times as many deaths.

Disproportionate numbers exist for other people of color across the United States, according to the Centers for Disease Control and Prevention (CDC). American Indians or Alaska Natives have 2.8 times as many cases of infection as Whites. Even worse, they have 5.3 times as many hospitalizations and 1.4 times as many deaths as Whites. African Americans have 2.6 times as many cases, 4.7 times as many hospitalizations, and 2.1 times as many deaths as Whites. Asian Americans have 1.1 times as many cases, 1.3 times as many hospitalizations, and the same ratio of deaths as Whites. "Every major crisis or catastrophe hits the most vulnerable communities the hardest,"[10] says Marc Morial, president and chief executive officer of the National Urban League, a civil rights organization that advocates on behalf of African Americans.

The differences in disease rates between the racial and ethnic groups does not have to do with race or ethnicity per se. Instead, they serve as markers of other factors that are different between racial or ethnic groups. One of the most important of these factors is increased exposure to the virus because of occupation. Not surprisingly, the virus spreads faster among essential workers than it does among those who can work at home and stay isolated. Henry Calderon did not work behind a desk in an office, which would allow him to work from home. He worked on construction sites. As a result, he was deemed an essential worker by his company. He most likely contracted the virus from someone else at the construction site. "This is our essential workforce," says Dr. Matt Willis, the public health officer for Marin County, referring to the Latino population. "This isn't the result of casual socializing at happy hour."[11] The same is true for other races and ethnic groups. "Black workers are more likely to hold the kinds of jobs that cannot be done from home,"[12] Morial points out.

"This is our essential workforce. This isn't the result of casual socializing at happy hour."[11]

—Dr. Matt Willis, the public health officer for Marin County, California

## A Chinese Superspreader Event

On January 19, 2020, 128 Buddhist worshippers boarded two buses for a fifty-minute ride to a temple in Ningbo, a city in China. Each bus had an air-conditioning unit that circulated the air inside the vehicle. Although the COVID-19 outbreak had begun in Wuhan, that city was hundreds of miles away, and no one on the buses wore masks. When the worshippers reached Ningbo, they joined about two hundred other people for a two-and-a-half-hour outdoor service and a lunch that was held indoors. They then returned to their buses for the ride home.

Within two weeks twenty-three of the sixty people on one bus tested positive for COVID-19. None of the people on the other bus became ill. Researchers later found that one of the people who got sick had recently had dinner with friends from Hubei Province, the epicenter of the COVID-19 outbreak. The sixty-four-year-old woman felt ill the day before the outing. She took medicine but did not suspect that she had COVID-19. She was the index case. The researchers found that even people seated far from the woman became ill. This case provided early evidence that the virus was transmitted not just through large droplets but also by airborne aerosols.

## Risks for Frontline Workers

Many frontline health care workers caring for COVID-19 patients are also people of color. For example, Filipinos make up less than 4 percent of California's population, but they constitute 20 percent of the state's registered nurses. These nurses often work in intensive care units and other acute care units, where they come into contact with COVID-19 patients. "Nursing intrinsically requires being in close quarters with patients, and there is no way you can do six-feet social distancing,"[13] says Dr. VJ Periyakoil, director of the Stanford Aging and Ethnogeriatrics Research Center, which studies the links between ethnicity and health.

Working on the front lines can be dangerous. A study by Kaiser Health News and the *Guardian* has found that 62 percent of frontline health care workers who have died from COVID-19 were people of color—Black, Latino, Asian/Pacific Islander, or Native American. In addition, 30.5 percent of the victims were born outside the United States. "Both figures support findings that people of color and immigrants (regardless of race) are dying at higher rates than their white and U.S.-born counterparts,"[14] states the report.

Other studies support these findings. Researchers at Harvard Medical School and King's College London looked at 2 million COVID-19 cases in the United States and the United Kingdom and found that 2,747 out of every 100,000 health care workers tested positive for COVID-19. This rate is ten times higher than the rate for the general population (242 cases per 100,000 people). The higher rate of infection among frontline health care workers is to be expected because of their exposure to the virus. But the researchers also found that health care workers of color were almost twice as likely to test positive for the coronavirus as their White counterparts. "If you think to yourself, 'Healthcare workers should be on equal footing in the workplace,' our study really showed that's definitely not the case,"[15] says Andrew Chan, an epidemiologist at Harvard and Massachusetts General Hospital and a coauthor of the study.

> "If you think to yourself, 'Healthcare workers should be on equal footing in the workplace,' our study really showed that's definitely not the case."[15]
>
> —Andrew Chan, an epidemiologist at Harvard and Massachusetts General Hospital

One of the reasons for the different health care worker infection rates is that people of color are more likely to care for patients with COVID-19. They also are more likely to work with inadequate protective gear, referred to as personal protective equipment (PPE). "Ensuring the adequate allocation of PPE is important to alleviate structural inequities in COVID-19 risk,"[16] state the researchers. Utibe Essien, a doctor in the VA Pittsburgh Healthcare System who studies health care practices, finds the unequal distribution of PPE disturbing. "I'm not surprised by these findings, but I'm disappointed by the result,"[17] he says.

## Income and Infection

Economic factors also contribute to the higher rates of COVID-19 among people of color. According to a 2019 report by the Brookings Institution, 63 percent of Latino workers and 54 percent of Black workers earn low wages, categorized as a median pay of $10.22 per hour or $17,950 per year. This compares to just 40 percent of Asian American workers and 37 percent of White workers. To compensate for having lower incomes, people of color often cut their housing costs by sharing homes or apartments with extended family or friends. Such living arrangements "can easily translate one case of COVID-19 into five or 10,"[18] says Marin County's Willis.

People who work in low-wage jobs, including janitorial, housekeeping, and restaurant employees, often do not have sick days. If staying home means losing needed income, these workers are likely to stay on the job even when they do not feel well. "If you're poor . . . you'll be working on daily-wage or low-paying jobs, which require you to go into work," says Periyakoil. "When you're forced to go into work, forced to be in contact, forced to take public transport, the nature of your finances imposes certain realities and restrictions on your daily life that put you at risk for higher stress and infections including COVID."[19]

It is not only that poor people need to work, it is also the kind of work they do. Many work in jobs at meatpacking plants, poultry plants, and warehouses, where it is difficult to avoid airborne viruses. "When you have people standing right next to each other working heavily—because of course this is a difficult job—and breathing heavily, you have a chance for spreading virus from just one infected individual to many that are in close proximity," says Tara Smith, a professor of epidemiology at Kent State University. "And then of course you have a chain of dominoes after that."[20] In July 2020 the CDC announced findings gathered from the health

*Workers typically stand shoulder to shoulder in a poultry plant (pictured). When the pandemic struck, many workers in plants like this one in Pennsylvania became infected with the coronavirus.*

departments in twenty-three states. The health departments reported that 16,233 workers in 239 meat and poultry plants had developed COVID-19, and 86 of those workers had died. A majority of the infected workers (87 percent) were racial or ethnic minorities.

After the CDC announced its findings, Senators Cory Booker and Elizabeth Warren launched an investigation into the meatpacking industry. They sent letters to meatpacking firms, asking for statistics on how many workers had become ill from COVID-19, how many had been hospitalized, and how many had died in each facility. They also asked the companies to list when they implemented the CDC's best practice guidelines to protect meat and poultry workers during the pandemic. These measures included slowing production lines, putting physical barriers between staff, making everybody wear face coverings, and paying employees who need to self-isolate.

Some companies had already implemented most of the recommendations. For example, Smithfield Foods, the world's largest pork producer, provided paid leave for employees most at risk—those age sixty or above—and had paid more than eleven thousand employees who had been exposed to the virus to stay home and self-quarantine. The company provided employees with free COVID-19 testing, erected barriers where social distancing was not possible, and issued PPE to the employees. Had all such companies done this, many lives could probably have been saved.

## Food Insecurity and Disease

Poor diet, while not in itself a factor in how COVID-19 spreads, does play a role in a person's susceptibility to the disease. People who have a high-fat, high-sugar diet are more likely to develop diabetes, heart disease, and other conditions that have been identified as major risk factors for illness and death from COVID-19. In the United States many people of color live in low-income areas with poor access to healthy foods. These areas are defined by the US Department of Agriculture (USDA) as food deserts. The USDA estimates that 23.5 million Americans live in food deserts.

People living in food deserts are not suffering from severe malnutrition. Instead, they are facing food insecurity, which a 2020 report by the White House Conference on Food, Nutrition and Health defines as "the limited or uncertain availability of nutritionally adequate and safe foods and beverages."[21] Filled with convenience stores and fast-food restaurants, food deserts have an overabundance of canned and packaged foods high in fat, sugar, and salt. Consuming these foods can be a matter of survival for low-income families. "I think it's really important to understand that dietary choices aren't moral choices," says Dr. Chinara Tate, director of nutrition at Mount Sinai Center of Excellence in Eating and Weight Disorders in New York. "If you have the option of purchasing an onion for a dollar or purchasing a meal for a dollar, it makes the most sense to purchase the meal, even if it's not the healthiest option because an onion is not going to feed your family."[22]

Research shows that preexisting conditions caused by poor diet and other factors are widespread among African Americans, Latinos, and other people of color. Fully 89 percent of people who have been hospitalized for COVID-19 have had at least one chronic preexisting condition. "We know that [poor diet] results in chronic diseases such as diabetes, high blood pressure and obesity," says Dr. Jessie Marshall, an assistant professor of internal medicine at the University of Michigan Medical School. "So again, COVID-19 did not create these racial disparities that we are seeing. It simply magnified these disparities in unbelievable ways."[23]

> "COVID-19 did not create these racial disparities that we are seeing. It simply magnified these disparities in unbelievable ways."[23]
>
> —Dr. Jessie Marshall, an assistant professor of internal medicine at the University of Michigan Medical School

People consuming high-fat and high-sugar foods often develop a condition known as metabolic syndrome. People with metabolic syndrome have excess fat around the middle, high blood pressure, high blood sugar, and a poor cholesterol profile. One problem with metabolic syndrome is that it suppresses the immune system, which is needed to fight off COVID-19. As a result, people with metabolic syndrome are more susceptible to becoming seriously ill if they contract the virus. Metabolic syndrome is also associated with low-grade, body-wide inflammation. Adding COVID-19's inflammation to this existing inflammation increases the risk of death for those who contract the virus. "Covid kills by causing an overwhelming inflammatory response that disables

People who eat a lot of high-fat, high-sugar foods often have problems with blood pressure, blood sugar, and cholesterol. These conditions make them more likely to develop serious illness if they contract COVID-19.

the body's ability to fight off pathogens,"[24] says Dr. Dariush Mozaffarian, dean of the Friedman School of Nutrition Science and Policy at Tufts University.

Metabolic syndrome and other preexisting conditions are a special problem for people of color because they have less access to medical care than Whites do. According to the US Department of Health and Human Services, 75.4 percent of White Americans had private health insurance in 2017, compared to just 55.5 percent of African Americans. That same year, 43.9 percent of African Americans relied on Medicaid or public health insurance, and 9.9 percent were uninsured. Many of the uninsured wait too long to see a doctor when they have COVID-19 symptoms. "I've seen my own family go through the fact that when you don't have health insurance you basically avoid the doctor until it's like a life-or-death scenario,"[25] says Belinda Archibong, assistant professor of economics at Columbia University's Barnard College. When people wait to get treatment, their chances of surviving COVID-19 go down.

COVID-19 has spread further and faster than any disease in history. In part that is because modern transportation has allowed for widespread travel of infected people during the pandemic. In part it is because the virus has long incubation and latency periods that make it difficult to identify and isolate carriers of the disease. And finally, a number of social and economic factors make it impossible for many people, especially low-income people, to avoid the virus and receive care for the disease once they get it. "It's the perfect storm," says Adrian De Leon, an assistant professor of American studies and ethnicity at the University of Southern California. "In terms of exposure to the pandemic, exposure to the virus, but also exposure to a lot of other factors, too."[26]

# CHAPTER THREE

# How COVID-19 Can Be Slowed

As scientists and medical professionals became aware of COVID-19, they tried to prevent the disease from spreading. Understanding that the disease was caused by a virus similar to SARS and MERS, they attempted to use the same techniques that controlled those outbreaks in 2002 and 2012, respectively. Those techniques—mainly, identifying the infected patients and isolating them from others—did not work as well for COVID-19. The rapid spread of COVID-19 has forced governments to adopt a wider array of containment measures. One of these measures is known as contact tracing.

## Contact Tracing

On July 1, 2020, Maggie Prosser, a senior at Ohio University in Athens, Ohio, was contacted by a state health department employee. Prosser says she was notified that a person with whom she had "a brief, non-socially distanced encounter"[27] at a friend's house had tested positive for COVID-19. The health official was doing contact tracing; that is, identifying and notifying everyone who has come in close contact with a person known to have a contagious and potentially deadly virus. The health department worker advised Prosser to isolate herself from others, or self-quarantine, for fourteen days. "Within two hours, I zoomed down U.S. Route 33 toward Athens, Ohio and away from my parents' house in downtown Columbus," Prosser remembers. "A two-week

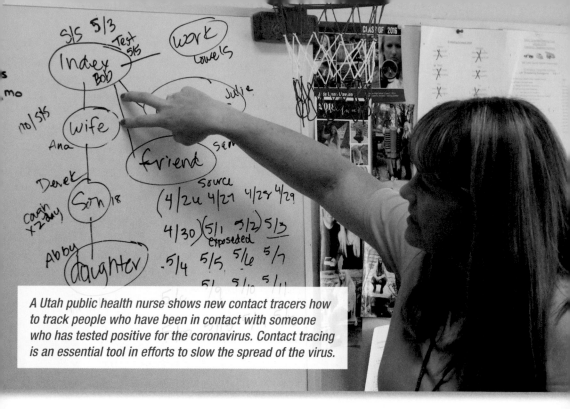

A Utah public health nurse shows new contact tracers how to track people who have been in contact with someone who has tested positive for the coronavirus. Contact tracing is an essential tool in efforts to slow the spread of the virus.

stock of groceries in tow, I was going to carry out my mandated quarantine in my dormant college apartment."[28]

Naturally, Prosser wanted to know whether she had the virus. That night she called her family doctor. He told her it was too soon for a test. If she had contracted the virus, it would take at least three days for the virus to multiply enough to be detected by the nasal swab test. Like the health department worker, the doctor told Prosser to watch for COVID-19 symptoms. Every day, a county health worker called to check on Prosser. Symptom-free for several days, Prosser asked the health worker if she could get a test before returning home. "The representative chastised me for considering returning home and plainly said the test was inaccurate and could produce false results," says Prosser. "After hanging up, I feverishly searched for nearby testing locations, all of which were backlogged and booked-up."[29]

Not knowing whether she had COVID-19 began to wear on Prosser. "Every sniffle and irregular heartbeat was anxiety producing, and sent me frantically searching for COVID-19 testing sites," she recalls. "Each relentless search turned up empty." When she finally spoke with a doctor via video call on the thirteenth day of her quarantine, Prosser was out of patience. "Saturday morning was filled with sorrowful tears as I sat in my stuffy, three-bedroom apartment pleading with a doctor to refer me for a test,"[30] she recalls. Because she had no symptoms, the doctor counseled against being tested. Later, Prosser spoke out about her experience. A journalism student, she wrote a commentary for the Ohio Capital Journal, criticizing the COVID-19 testing process:

> It is unrealistic for government officials to expect people to quarantine for 14 days every time they are exposed to COVID-19 without adequate and effective testing. It is unrealistic to expect people to live with the crippling and debilitating anxiety of not knowing whether or not you are sick. It is unrealistic for employees to feel safe returning to work without knowing if they could become symptomatic or not. But it is especially unrealistic for our state government to assume that we can slow the spread of this virus with our current diminutive and futile testing.[31]

Public health and infectious disease experts say that contact tracing and testing are vital to containing a pandemic. Unlike broad public measures, contact tracing focuses on those who are at immediate risk of the disease and are most likely to spread it. "The thing that's incredibly valuable about contact tracing at this point is the literal intelligence—the knowledge and understanding—that it gives decision-makers," says Danielle Allen, director of the Edmond J. Safra Center for Ethics at Harvard University and a coauthor of a handbook of COVID-19 policy. "If you can work out that you have a whole cluster coming from one specific kind

"Every sniffle and irregular heartbeat was anxiety producing, and sent me frantically searching for COVID-19 testing sites."[30]

—Maggie Prosser, an Ohio University student

of activity, then that's what you shut down—you don't have to shut down everything."[32]

Contact tracing can dramatically reduce the coronavirus infection rate, but only if the practice is widespread. Researchers at Stanford University found that contact tracing programs combined with effective testing and quarantining can reduce overall transmission rates by almost half. However, such programs can only work if detection of cases in the community and successful outreach to contacts both exceed 50 percent. A survey conducted by the Johns Hopkins Center for Health Security in collaboration with NPR found that the United States has only about half of the contact tracers needed to curb the pandemic. According to the survey, the total number of contact tracers was 53,116 in October 2020. That number was four times greater than the number of contact tracers working in April, but it was still far short of the 100,000 experts said were needed nationwide. Only two states—Vermont and Oregon—and the District of Columbia had enough contact tracers to meet the needs of the population. Four other states—Hawaii, Maine, Montana, and New York—had enough contact tracers when the state's reserve staff was included. The other forty-four states did not have enough contact tracers available.

## Social Distancing

Without sufficient contact tracing, public health officials have no choice but to call for the entire population to take steps to curb the spread of the virus. Understanding that many of the people who had contracted the virus might not know they have it, either because the disease was in the incubation period or the person was asymptomatic, public health officials called for people to remain at least 6 feet (1.8 m) apart when in public. This practice is known as social distancing. The idea is that an infected person shedding the virus through speaking, coughing, or sneezing would not project droplets or aerosols in great enough numbers to infect another person beyond a 4- to 5-foot (1.2 to 1.5 m) radius.

## COVID-Sniffing Dogs

Passengers leaving the baggage area of Helsinki Airport in Finland are given a disposable wipe and asked to wipe their neck for a voluntary COVID-19 test. Health workers take the box containing the perspiration sample behind a nearby wall, where a trainer waits with a dog. If the person has COVID-19—even if he or she has no symptoms—the dog will pick the sample out of a lineup within ten seconds. According to researchers, the dogs are right 94 percent of the time. Passengers who test positive for COVID-19 are directed to a medical office in the airport. The entire process takes a minute or less.

Dogs, which possess a sense of smell estimated to be ten thousand to one hundred thousand times keener than that of humans, have been used for years to detect hypoglycemia in diabetics and some kinds of cancer. COVID-sniffing dogs are also being used to screen passengers at airports in the United Arab Emirates. Virpi Perala, a representative of Evidensia, a company that funded the Helsinki research, believes dogs could be used to screen for the virus in retirement homes, schools, and malls, but seven hundred to one thousand disease-sniffing dogs would be needed. "We could keep our country open if we had enough dogs," Perala says.

Quoted in Elian Peltier, "The Nose Needed for This Coronavirus Test Isn't Yours. It's a Dog's," *New York Times*, September 23, 2020. www.nytimes.com.

Businesses and government offices quickly adopted the policy, often marking their floors with tape or stickers located 6 feet (1.8 m) apart to show people where to stand when they lined up at a cash register or other point of service. People were encouraged to practice social distancing at all times and situations—while on walks, pumping gas at the gas station, or even meeting friends socially. Hugs, handshakes, and air kisses became a thing of the past.

## Face Masks

After the superspreading event at the Skagit Valley Chorale in March 2020, epidemiologists understood that the COVID-19 virus can spread easily through the air. As a result, they began to call for people not only to practice social distancing but also to wear a face mask when in public. The idea of a mask is not that it will protect the wearer from aerosol-borne viruses but that it might prevent infected individuals from shedding large amounts of virus through their nose and mouth, thereby reducing the likelihood of further spread.

Eager to play their part in reducing the spread of COVID-19, most people went along with the mask requirements, despite the lack of comfort in wearing them, the difficulty of breathing through them, and the inconvenience of having to repeat things they said because the mask muffled their speech. Some turned their masks into fashion statements, buying and wearing masks imprinted with cartoon character designs, animal snouts, monster mouths, or funny sayings. Some posted cartoons and memes about COVID-19 masks in social media.

*At the urging of public health officials, many people have worn masks when social distancing was not possible. Despite evidence that masks help to prevent the virus's spread, some people have refused to comply.*

Some people were not pleased about having to wear a mask. Many questioned the science behind the new requirements. They remembered that US surgeon general Jerome Adams, the operational head of the US Public Health Service Commissioned Corps, stated at the beginning of the pandemic that nonsurgical masks were useless against the virus. Adams and others were basing their recommendations on science done up to that point. A 2006 study done for the CDC entitled "Disease Mitigation Measures in the Control of Pandemic Influenza" concluded that plain surgical masks, let alone nonsurgical cloth masks, were not effective in preventing the spread of disease. The researchers wrote:

> Studies have shown that the ordinary surgical mask does little to prevent inhalation of small droplets bearing influenza virus. The pores in the mask become blocked by moisture from breathing, and the air stream simply diverts around the mask. There are few data available to support the efficacy of N95 or surgical masks outside a healthcare setting.[33]

## Questioning the Motives Behind the Mandates

Believing the science that face masks do not protect wearers from COVID-19 and reasoning that healthy people cannot spread the virus, critics of the masks began to probe the motives of the mask mandates. Some argued that governors who mandated the use of masks were more concerned with scoring political points than savings lives, ordering the mask mandates only for appearance's sake. Others saw a darker motive behind the mask mandates. They claimed that one purpose for mask requirements was to extend the government's authority into people's everyday lives, stripping them of their individual rights and preparing them for even greater infringements on their liberty in the future. Adams tried to quell these doubts by explaining that the mandates were based on lessons learned from the pandemic. Adams said on the CBS program *Face the Nation*:

> Up to 50 percent of people who can spread this disease, spread it without having symptoms. And that's why the American people need to know that science is about giving the best recommendations you can—and when you learn more, you change those recommendations. Our recommendations have changed. . . . Now, people of America, [it is] important to know you should wear a face covering."[34]

For additional protection against the spread of the disease, some public and private offices installed clear plastic barriers in heavily trafficked areas, such as grocery checkout stations and bank teller windows. These were not substitutes for masks; rather, they were used in addition to masks. The idea was that people could have face-to-face encounters with less risk of virus-laden droplets crossing from one personal space to another. Some offices and restaurants also installed the clear barriers to cut down on the spread of the virus.

## Closing Places of Business

The most drastic step taken to slow the pandemic was to close schools, government offices, and businesses. Although children were not at high risk of developing serious cases of COVID-19, the fear was that if schools remained open, the virus would be passed among them and carried home to infect adults.

Not all businesses or government offices were closed. Businesses deemed essential were allowed to remain open, as long as they followed guidelines for social distancing and mask wearing. On March 19, 2020, California governor Gavin Newsom ordered all Californians to stay home except to go to an essential job or to shop for essential needs. The next day New York governor Andrew Cuomo signed a similar order, requiring nonessential busi-

# The WHO's Case Against Lockdowns

In an October 2020 interview with the British magazine the *Spectator*, Dr. David Nabarro, the WHO's special envoy on COVID-19, explains why his organization is against government lockdowns.

> We in the World Health Organization do not advocate lockdowns as the primary means of control of this virus. The only time we believe a lockdown is justified is to buy you time to reorganize, regroup, rebalance your resources, protect your health workers who are exhausted, but by and large, we'd rather not do it. . . .
>
> Look what's happened to . . . farmers all over the world because their markets have got dented. Look what's happening to poverty levels. It seems that we may well have a doubling of world poverty by next year. We may well have at least a doubling of child malnutrition. . . .
>
> This is a terrible, ghastly global catastrophe, actually, and so we really do appeal to all world leaders: Stop using lockdown as your primary control method. Develop better systems for doing it. Work together and learn from each other, but remember, lockdowns just have one consequence that you must never ever belittle, and that is making poor people an awful lot poorer.

Quoted in Andrew Neil, "The Week in 60 Minutes #6—with Andrew Neil and WHO Covid-19 Envoy David Nabarro," YouTube, October 8, 2020. https://youtu.be/x8oH7cBxgwE.

nesses to close statewide. Businesses deemed essential in both states included those in health care; transportation; infrastructure, such as utilities; manufacturing of essential items; retail, including grocery stores and pharmacies; services, such as trash and recycling collection, building cleaning and maintenance, and auto repair; financial institutions; construction; and services necessary for maintaining safety, including law enforcement, fire response, and emergency response.

Businesses that involved casual gatherings of fifty people or more were considered nonessential and ordered to close. This included bars, restaurants, gyms, movie theaters, casinos, auditoriums, concerts, conferences, sporting events, and physical fitness centers. Houses of worship were not at first ordered to close, but New York strongly recommended that services not be held and social distance be maintained at any activities.

Many businesses remained open but allowed the employees to work from home to prevent the spread of the virus in the workplace. Some of these companies already allowed employees to telecommute, or work from home using a computer connection to the office. Almost overnight, entire workforces were telecommuting. Companies scrambled to get videoconferencing and file-sharing software to all employees so they could communicate with each other and carry on their work. Some businesses purchased new devices such as laptops and tablets so employees could work from home. Many purchased additional security software so files could not be hacked as they were shared online.

> "The rapid and massive shift to remote learning in the spring . . . revealed that access to Wi-Fi and digital devices at home remains inadequate for millions of U.S. households."[35]
>
> —Mark Lieberman, a contributing writer for *Education Week*

## Closing the Schools

Students were also displaced. Schools all across the country closed to limit the spread of the virus, and millions of students were required to log on to computers and other devices for remote learning. Like the virus itself, distance learning has been particularly difficult for low-income students. "The rapid and massive shift to remote learning in the spring . . . revealed that access to Wi-Fi and digital devices at home remains inadequate for millions of U.S. households; and many schools lack the technological infrastructure or resources to ensure all students can learn online,"[35] observed Mark Lieberman, a contributing writer for *Education Week*.

When schools reopened in the fall, some offered full-time classes, but most used a hybrid model, a mixture of in-person and online instruction. In addition, a large number of parents applied to homeschool their children, fearing that the schools would not be safe until a vaccine was found or the disease had run its course. "I'm very pro-school and very pro-public school, and I never thought I would be thinking about home-schooling," says Jessica Bates, a freelance writer and a mother of two in Nashville, Tennessee. "But with COVID-19 spreading and my state opening back up as cases are rising, we're concerned with my son going to school."[36]

> "I'm very pro-school and very pro-public school, and I never thought I would be thinking about home-schooling. But with COVID-19 spreading and my state opening back up as cases are rising, we're concerned with my son going to school."[36]
>
> —Jessica Bates, a freelance writer and mother of two

## Testing for the Virus

Perhaps the most important step governments can take to stop the spread of a disease like COVID-19 is to test the population to see who has the virus and where they are located. Those who have contracted the disease can then be separated from healthy people, even by quarantine in the home, so they do not give it to anyone else. The problem with COVID-19 is that so many people can carry the disease without having symptoms that it is hard to identify them and isolate them.

When the new virus first was identified, no one had any testing kits to identify whether a person had contracted the virus. Chinese scientists quickly identified the genome—the complete genetic code—for the virus. They sent the information to laboratories around world so they could create a test to see whether the virus was present in a person's tissues. Within days of receiving the genetic sequence from China, the CDC began to produce viable tests. The first batch of tests worked well, but a second batch, released on February 5, 2020, was contaminated and did

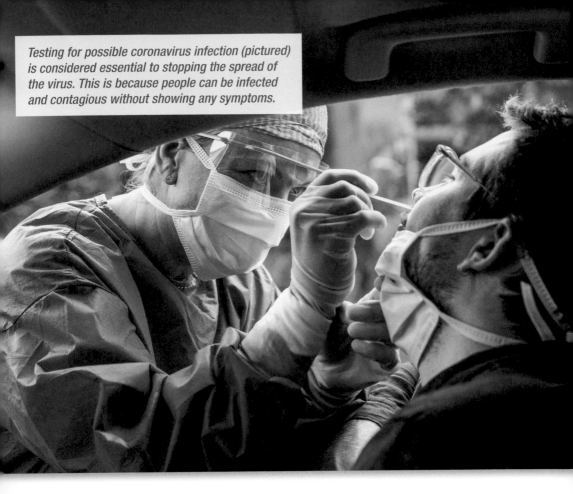

*Testing for possible coronavirus infection (pictured) is considered essential to stopping the spread of the virus. This is because people can be infected and contagious without showing any symptoms.*

not work as designed. As a result, the laboratories trying to process the patient samples had to ship them to the CDC for an accurate analysis. To make matters worse, the US Food and Drug Administration's (FDA) rules governing the creation of test kits prevented commercial and academic labs from developing their own tests for the virus. The FDA reversed this policy on February 29, but valuable testing time had already been lost.

Other labs quickly developed their own tests and applied for approval by the FDA. Not realizing the length of the incubation period or the time a person can be asymptomatic, public health officials encouraged only people with severe COVID-19 symptoms to get tested. By May 11 the CDC reported that it had tested 6,275 specimens and other labs had tested 818,682 specimens. This was still too few tests to identify pockets of the outbreak, however. Scientists said that ten people have to be tested for every person who tests positive for the virus. Soon states were encouraging asymptomatic people to get tested. By September an average of 725,000 tests were being performed per day, but this was just 66 percent of the number needed to stop the spread of the virus. According to the Harvard Global Health Institute, at least 1.1 million tests need to be conducted per day to be able to contain the pandemic.

By the end of October, well over 44 million people worldwide had contracted coronavirus. The number of cases in the United States alone was approaching 9 million, or about 84,000 new cases per day. That represented a significant jump from the previous high point of nearly 75,000 cases per day in July. For people worldwide, a safe and effective vaccine represents the best hope of halting the virus's spread. However, experts believe that many of the mitigation efforts will remain in place even after the population is vaccinated.

# CHAPTER FOUR

# How COVID-19 Can Be Stopped

Contact tracing, virus testing, social distancing, and mask wearing are all measures that can restrain the spread of COVID-19, but they cannot stop it completely. A viral disease like COVID-19 can only be stopped in one of two ways. Either large numbers of people acquire natural immunity to the disease, or a vaccine is developed that immunizes a similar portion of the population. When a large majority of a population is immune to a viral disease, the virus cannot find new hosts, and it dies out.

## Herd Immunity

The condition when a large group of people in one area become immune to a disease, making its further spread unlikely, is known as herd immunity. With herd immunity, the disease may not disappear completely, but the infection rate is so low that it is no longer a public health crisis. "I think with a good combination of good public health measures, a degree of global herd immunity, and a good vaccine, which I do hope and feel cautiously optimistic we will get, I think when you put all three of those together we will get very good control of this," said Anthony Fauci in July 2020. "Whether it's this year or next year, I'm not certain."[37]

When a community achieves herd immunity, everyone is protected, even those who have not had the disease and are not immune to it themselves. In modern times, herd immunity has often been achieved through vaccination. For example, on May 8, 1980, nearly two centuries after English biologist Edward Jenner developed a vaccine for smallpox—the first vaccine of any kind—the United Nations World Health Assembly officially declared that smallpox had been eradicated. Scientists believe that because COVID-19 spreads so easily, roughly 60 to 70 percent of the population needs to be immune to the disease before herd immunity can be achieved. In the United States the number of immune people needed to achieve herd immunity is about 200 million.

## The Swedish Experiment

When COVID-19 first emerged, some scientists advocated letting it spread through the population to naturally create herd immunity. They reasoned that since the disease was less dangerous to people under fifty years old, it made sense to leave schools and businesses open. According to this line of thinking, letting children and younger adults catch the disease would eventually lead to herd immunity. At the same time, precautions could be taken to prevent older people and those with risk factors from being exposed to the virus.

The danger with the herd immunity approach is that many people must become ill for it to work, and this includes children. "Anyone who has been on the front lines of this pandemic in a children's hospital can tell you we've taken care of lots of kids that are very sick," says Sean O'Leary, vice chair of the American Academy of Pediatrics committee on infectious diseases. "Yes, it's less severe in children than adults, but it's not completely benign."[38] Without an effective treatment for COVID-19, some of those who become sick would die.

Government officials worldwide had to decide whether to try to minimize the spread of COVID-19 or allow it to spread through the population in hopes of creating herd immunity. Sweden opted for the latter, allowing the virus to run its course. The government did not order any kind of lockdown. It banned gatherings of more than fifty people, but it allowed schools and businesses to remain open. Even without laws and mandates, the people of Sweden practiced social distancing and wore masks. "Voluntary restrictions work as well as legal ones,"[39] says Anders Tegnell, Sweden's chief epidemiologist.

Sweden's experiment resulted in higher infection rates and more deaths than in other countries in the region. As of August 2020, Sweden had 8,200 confirmed COVID-19 cases per million people. This compares to just 1,780 per million in neighboring Norway and 2,560 in nearby Denmark. It is even higher than the rate in the United Kingdom, which enacted restrictions later than many other countries. It is, however, lower than the rate in the United States, which was 15,400 cases per million people as of that date.

The death rate in Sweden was higher than in neighboring countries as well. Sweden saw 57 COVID-19 deaths per 100,000 people, a rate 11 times higher than that of Norway, which had just 5 deaths per 100,000 people. The rate was 5 times greater than

In the spring of 2020, when many countries were in lockdown, Sweden allowed businesses to remain open. The government's effort to create herd immunity resulted in higher infection and death rates than in other nearby countries.

Denmark's rate of 11 per 100,000. The death rate was almost as high as the death rate in the United States (61 per 100,000), even though the United States had nearly twice as many cases per 100,000 people. Among countries in northern and western Europe, only the United Kingdom, with a death rate of 63 per 100,000, had a higher death rate.

Despite the higher case and death rates, Sweden did not come close to achieving herd immunity. Only about 20 percent of the people in Sweden's capital, Stockholm, contracted the disease. This was far short of the 60 to 70 percent level needed to achieve herd immunity.

## Acquired Immunity

One of the concerns with achieving herd immunity is whether people will form an immunity to the disease once they have been infected. Normally, some of the body's T cells will recognize a pathogen that has invaded the body before. The T cells will then signal disease-fighting B cells to destroy the pathogen. This is known as acquired immunity. (The body also has innate immunity that employs white blood cells to fight pathogens.)

The body does not always form an immunity to a disease. Sometimes it does, but the acquired immunity is short lived. When COVID-19 emerged, scientists did not know whether people would develop an immunity to the disease or how long that immunity might last. If the body did not develop an immunity, or if it were short lived, it would be unlikely that a community would develop herd immunity.

A study in Iceland published in the *New England Journal of Medicine* in September 2020 offered hope that COVID-19 survivors would develop an acquired immunity. The researchers measured the antibodies in blood samples from 30,576 people in Iceland, including 1,215 who had recovered from COVID-19. They found that antibodies to COVID-19 were present in more than 91 percent of those recovering from the disease. The study did not establish whether the antibodies present would stop the disease

"What we don't know is really the million-dollar question: How do these antibodies reflect immunity against this virus and inhibition of this virus."[40]

—Jason Kindrachuk, an assistant professor of medical microbiology and infectious diseases at the University of Manitoba

from recurring. "What we don't know is really the million-dollar question: How do these antibodies reflect immunity against this virus and inhibition of this virus," says Jason Kindrachuk, an assistant professor of medical microbiology and infectious diseases at the University of Manitoba in Winnipeg. "Just because you see antibodies being produced, it doesn't tell you that those antibodies are going to act specifically against the virus."[40]

## Creating a Vaccine

The stability of the COVID-19 antibodies was a good sign that a vaccine could be developed. A vaccine triggers an immune reaction against a disease without the person actually having to get the disease. Most vaccines use noninfectious disease cells—either dead cells or altered cells—to trigger an immune response.

The most common way for vaccine makers to create a vaccine is to use the virus that causes the common cold, known as the adenovirus. The vaccine makers remove the proteins that make the adenovirus infectious and then add proteins that are unique to the disease they are trying to stop. In the case of COVID-19, they add the protein spikes that give the coronavirus its name. This vaccine virus can invade cells, but it cannot make copies of itself. When this harmless virus is injected into a healthy patient, the body will react to it, attack it, and destroy it. The T cells will retain a "memory" of the profile of the defeated invader. If the vaccinated person is exposed to the real COVID-19 virus later, the body will recognize the virus's unique spike protein and trigger a targeted immune response. This response will wipe out the invading cells before there are enough of them to make the person sick. If enough people have the vaccine, the disease cannot spread through the population.

## Operation Warp Speed

After Chinese scientists identified the genetic code of the COVID-19 coronavirus on January 7, 2020, pharmaceutical companies, university laboratories, and government research centers began working on a vaccine for COVID-19. Following a March 2, 2020, roundtable meeting at the White House, the Trump administration began to form public-private partnerships to develop a vaccine as quickly as possible. On March 30 the US Department of Health and Human Services (HHS) announced that it was awarding $456 million in funds to pharmaceutical giant Johnson & Johnson for the development of a vaccine candidate.

## Manipulating Genes to Make a Vaccine

While some vaccine makers use modified adenoviruses to create a vaccine, others use the relatively new process of gene manipulation. Every cell of an organism contains molecules called DNA. These molecules contain the genetic instructions for the development, functioning, growth, and reproduction of the cell. Another molecule known as RNA carries these instructions to the machinery of the cell. To make a vaccine, scientists remove part of the RNA from a disease virus and inject it into a person. The RNA is not infectious itself, but it contains instructions for the body to make proteins similar to those of the disease-causing pathogen. These proteins are known as antigens. For COVID-19 the RNA snippets tell the body to create the virus's spike protein. When the body makes these antigens, the immune system recognizes them as invaders and produces molecules known as antibodies to destroy them. The immune system retains enough of these antibodies to recognize the antigens of the actual pathogen, should it ever invade the body. This "memory" of the antigen gives the body acquired immunity to the pathogen. RNA vaccines can be developed quickly, because they only require reading, snipping, and purifying the pathogen's genetic code.

On April 29, 2020, several news organizations revealed the existence of Operation Warp Speed, a multiagency government operation working with pharmaceutical companies to accelerate the development of COVID-19 countermeasures. These countermeasures included the manufacturing and distribution of a COVID-19 vaccine. On May 15 President Donald Trump formally announced Operation Warp Speed, stating that the goal was to produce and deliver 300 million doses of safe and effective vaccines, with the initial doses available by January 2021.

Over the next several months, the HHS awarded more than $7 billion in support to pharmaceutical companies working on vaccines. These companies include Moderna ($483 million), AstraZeneca ($1.2 billion), Novavax ($1.6 billion), Pfizer ($1.95 billion), and GlaxoSmithKline ($2 billion). "Through Operation Warp Speed, we are assembling a portfolio of vaccines to increase the odds that the American people will have at least one safe, effective vaccine as soon as the end of this year,"[41] HHS secretary Alex Azar said on July 22, 2020.

> "Through Operation Warp Speed, we are assembling a portfolio of vaccines to increase the odds that the American people will have at least one safe, effective vaccine as soon as the end of this year."[41]
>
> —Alex Azar, the secretary of health and human services

## The First COVID-19 Vaccines

Other nations have also been working on a vaccine at warp speed. On June 25, 2020, the Chinese government announced that its Central Military Commission had approved a COVID-19 vaccine for use by the Chinese military. According to a statement by vaccine maker CanSino Biologics, which developed the vaccine jointly with the Beijing Institute of Biotechnology, the vaccine appeared safe and had the potential to prevent COVID-19.

The Chinese vaccine did produce side effects, as vaccines often do. In the vaccine's initial trials, about half of the vaccine recipients developed a fever. According to a study by the vaccine devel-

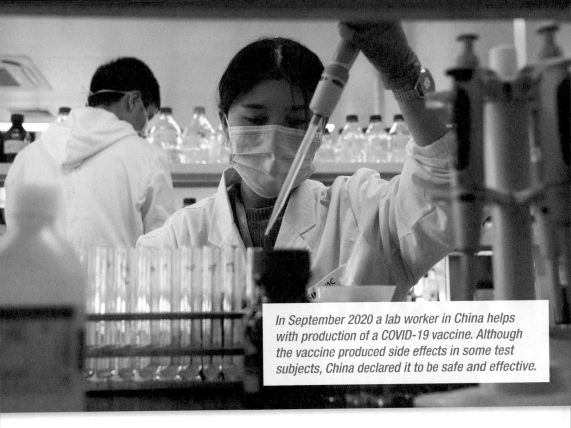

In September 2020 a lab worker in China helps with production of a COVID-19 vaccine. Although the vaccine produced side effects in some test subjects, China declared it to be safe and effective.

opers that was published in *The Lancet* on May 20, 2020, about 44 percent of the vaccine recipients said they had a fever, and 39 percent reported having a headache after receiving the vaccine. Nine percent of the people in the trial said their side effects were so severe that they prevented normal activity.

On August 11, 2020, the Russian Federation announced that it had approved a vaccine against COVID-19. Russian president Vladimir Putin made the announcement, stating, "I know [the vaccine] works quite effectively, helps to develop strong immunity, and has gone through all the necessary tests." To emphasize his confidence in the safety of the vaccine, Putin said that his own daughter had received the vaccine. "She feels well, and the concentration of antibodies is high," the Russian president said. "The main thing is to ensure unconditional safety and effectiveness of this vaccine in the future."[42] The Russian government estimated that it would be able to produce 500 million doses of the vaccine per year.

Scientists outside Russia were skeptical of the announcement. They were concerned that the Russian government had

## The United States Refuses to Join Global Vaccine Initiative

In September 2020 the Trump administration applied its "America First" foreign policy to global efforts spearheaded by the WHO to distribute a COVID-19 vaccine. The United States, which began the process of formally withdrawing from the WHO in July 2020, joined Great Britain and Japan in contracting directly with vaccine developers to ensure their citizens are first in line to receive vaccines, a practice critics call "vaccine nationalism."

The WHO's COVID-19 Vaccine Global Access Facility, or COVAX, is aimed at distributing the vaccine equitably to the 170 countries, both rich and poor, that have joined the coalition. "What we need to persuade global leaders is that as a vaccine becomes available in these initially limited quantities, it needs to be shared globally, that it shouldn't be the case that just a handful of countries get all of the vaccine that is available in the first half of 2021," said Dr. Richard Hatchett, head of the Coalition for Epidemic Preparedness Innovations, which is part of COVAX. Some experts point out that the America First policy could backfire if American vaccine makers fail to produce an effective vaccine but countries participating in COVAX do. That would mean other countries would be first in line for the vaccine, and the United States would be last.

Quoted in Jennifer Rigby, "Blow to Global Efforts to Distribute Covid-19 Vaccine as Trump Refuses to Join WHO Scheme," *The Telegraph* (London), September 2, 2020. www.telegraph.co.uk.

approved the vaccine before it had even entered Phase 3 trials, when hundreds or even thousands of people receive the vaccine, testing its effectiveness outside the laboratory and ensuring that it is safe for all kinds of people. The Russian government approved the vaccine on the basis of limited testing trials. In one trial, seventy-six people received the vaccine. All of the participants developed a strong immune response. However, it was unknown whether this response will actually protect people. "Immune response might not be directly proportional to the degree of protection—you can only find this out in large-scale trials,"[43] observed Peter Openshaw, a professor of experimental medicine at Imperial College London.

In September 2020 Russia began large-scale Phase 3 trials of the vaccine. More than forty thousand people in Russia, India, the Philippines, Saudi Arabia, and the United Arab Emirates began receiving the vaccine.

## Raising the Standards for an American Vaccine

After the announcements of the Chinese and Russian vaccines, the Trump administration expressed optimism that an American vaccine could be available soon. Some scientists, politicians, and members of the public expressed concern that the administration might be pressuring the FDA to release a vaccine that had not been thoroughly tested for safety and effectiveness. In response, on October 6, 2020, the FDA issued its new guidance to vaccine makers regarding the scientific data and information that would be required before a COVID-19 vaccine could be approved. These tightened requirements, including increasing the length of the human vaccine trials, were designed to build public

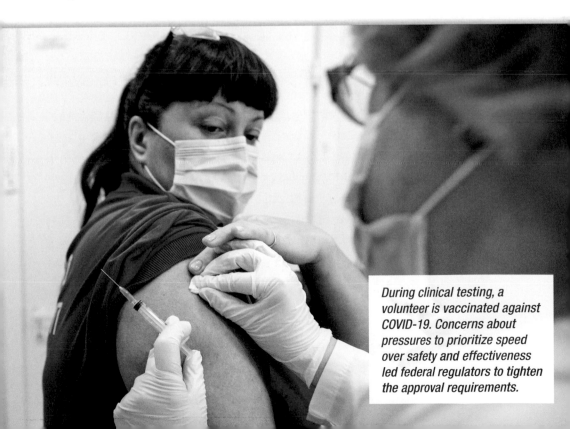

*During clinical testing, a volunteer is vaccinated against COVID-19. Concerns about pressures to prioritize speed over safety and effectiveness led federal regulators to tighten the approval requirements.*

confidence in the vaccine. Dr. Peter Marks, director of the FDA's Center for Biologics Evaluation and Research, explained:

> Being open and clear about the circumstances under which the issuance of an emergency use authorization for a COVID-19 vaccine would be appropriate is critical to building public confidence and ensuring the use of COVID-19 vaccines once available. . . . In addition to outlining our expectations for vaccine sponsors, we also hope the agency's guidance on COVID-19 vaccines helps the public understand our science-based decision-making process that assures vaccine quality, safety and efficacy for any vaccine that is authorized or approved.[44]

By September 2020 at least seventeen COVID-19 vaccines were in development around the world. It was still unclear whether any of them would prevent people from getting the disease in the real world. Anthony Fauci says it is unlikely that any of the vaccines being tested will be highly effective. "The chances of it being 98 percent effective is not great,"[45] Fauci says. Instead, scientists are hoping that a vaccine will be at least 75 percent effective. However, in its October guidance, the FDA said it will approve a COVID-19 vaccine if it is shown to be safe and prevented the disease in at least 50 percent of those receiving the vaccine. "We really felt strongly that that had to be the floor,"[46] says Dr. Stephen Hahn, the FDA's commissioner. Fifty percent protection is about what traditional influenza vaccines provide. If 50 percent of the population is protected against the virus, that would approach the level needed for herd immunity.

Even if one or more of the vaccines work and enable the world to achieve herd immunity, Fauci believes that COVID-19 will not disappear completely. "It is so efficient in its ability to transmit from human to human that I think we ultimately will get control of it," says Fauci. "I don't really see us eradicating it."[47] If that is the case, some of the steps taken to stop the spread of COVID-19 may be with the world for years, if not generations, to come.

## Introduction: Mass Killer

1. Joshua Lederberg, "Medical Science, Infectious Disease, and the Unity of Humankind," *Journal of the American Medical Association*, August 5, 1988. https://jamanetwork.com.
2. Quoted in Bernard Fields et al., eds., *Genetically Altered Viruses and the Environment*. Cold Spring Harbor, NY: Cold Spring Harbor Laboratory, 1985, p. 108.

## Chapter One: How COVID-19 Kills

3. Quoted in Laura Ungar, "Essential and in Danger: Coronavirus Sickens, Even Kills Public Health Workers," KHN, July 22, 2020. https://khn.org.
4. Quoted in Meredith Wadman et al., "How Does Coronavirus Kill? Clinicians Trace a Ferocious Rampage Through the Body, from Brain to Toes," *Science*, April 17, 2020. www.sciencemag.org.
5. Quoted in Wadman et al., "How Does Coronavirus Kill?"
6. Quoted in Sarah Gibbens, "Here's What COVID-19 Does to a Child's Body," National Geographic, July 24, 2020. www.nationalgeographic.com.

## Chapter Two: How COVID-19 Spreads

7. Quoted in Rachel Scheier, "Coronavirus: Latino Workers Hit Hard in Upscale Marin County," *Los Angeles Times*, August 10, 2020. www.latimes.com.
8. Nicholas Christakis, "Responding to Covid-19," *The Economist*, August 10, 2020. www.economist.com.
9. Shelly L. Miller et al., "Transmission of SARS-CoV-2 by Inhalation of Respiratory Aerosol in the Skagit Valley Chorale Superspreading Event," *Indoor Air*, June 15, 2020. www.medrxiv.org.
10. Quoted in Allison Aubrey, "Who's Hit Hardest by COVID-19? Why Obesity, Stress and Race All Matter," NPR, April 18, 2020. www.npr.org.
11. Quoted in Scheier, "Coronavirus."
12. Quoted in Aubrey, "Who's Hit Hardest by COVID-19?"
13. Quoted in Tiffany Wong, "Little Noticed, Filipino Americans Are Dying of COVID-19 at an Alarming Rate," *Los Angeles Times*, July 21, 2020. www.latimes.com.

14. Danielle Renwick and Shoshana Dubnow, "Many People of Color, Immigrants Among over 1,000 US Health Workers Lost to COVID," KHN, August 26, 2020. https://khn.org.
15. Quoted in Carolyn Crist, "COVID Hits Health Care Workers of Color Hardest," WebMD, August 20, 2020. www.webmd.com.
16. Quoted in Crist, "COVID Hits Health Care Workers of Color Hardest."
17. Quoted in Crist, "COVID Hits Health Care Workers of Color Hardest."
18. Quoted in Scheier, "Coronavirus."
19. Quoted in Wong, "Little Noticed, Filipino Americans Are Dying of COVID-19 at an Alarming Rate."
20. Quoted in Anthony Reuben, "Coronavirus: Why Have There Been So Many Outbreaks in Meat Processing Plants?," BBC, June 23, 2020. www.bbc.com.
21. Jerold Mande et al., *Report of the 50th Anniversary of the White House Conference on Food, Nutrition, and Health: Honoring the Past, Taking Actions for Our Future*. Boston: Tufts University, 2020, p. 12.
22. Quoted in Courtney Connley, "Racial Health Disparities Already Existed in America—the Coronavirus Just Exacerbated Them," CNBC, May 15, 2020. www.cnbc.com.
23. Quoted in Connley, "Racial Health Disparities Already Existed in America—the Coronavirus Just Exacerbated Them."
24. Quoted in Jane E. Brody, "How Poor Diet Contributes to Coronavirus Risk," *New York Times*, April 20, 2020. www.nytimes.com.
25. Quoted in Connley, "Racial Health Disparities Already Existed in America—the Coronavirus Just Exacerbated Them."
26. Quoted in Wong, "Little Noticed, Filipino Americans Are Dying of COVID-19 at an Alarming Rate."

## Chapter Three: How COVID-19 Can Be Slowed

27. Maggie Prosser, "I Was Exposed to COVID-19 and Couldn't Get Tested for 16 Days," Ohio Capital Journal, July 14, 2020. https://ohiocapitaljournal.com.
28. Prosser, "I Was Exposed to COVID-19 and Couldn't Get Tested for 16 Days."
29. Prosser, "I Was Exposed to COVID-19 and Couldn't Get Tested for 16 Days."
30. Prosser, "I Was Exposed to COVID-19 and Couldn't Get Tested for 16 Days."
31. Prosser, "I Was Exposed to COVID-19 and Couldn't Get Tested for 16 Days."
32. Quoted in Selena Simmons-Duffin, "COVID-19 Contact Tracing Workforce Barely 'Inching Up' as Cases Surge," NPR, October 14, 2020. www.npr.org.

33. Thomas V. Inglesby et al., "Disease Mitigation Measures in the Control of Pandemic Influenza," *Biosecurity and Bioterrorism: Biodefense Strategy, Practice, and Science*, vol. 4, no. 4, 2006, p. 372.

34. Quoted in CBS News, "Transcript: Surgeon General Jerome Adams on 'Face the Nation,'" July 12, 2020. www.cbsnews.com.

35. Mark Lieberman, "COVID-19 & Remote Learning: How to Make It Work," *Education Week*, July 22, 2020. www.edweek.org.

36. Quoted in Safia Samee Ali, "Parents Are Opting to Home School Their Children Because of COVID-19, but Experts Say It Might Not Be for Everyone," NBC News, July 5, 2020. www.nbcnews.com.

## Chapter Four: How COVID-19 Can Be Stopped

37. Quoted in Jessie Hellmann, "Fauci on Coronavirus: 'I Don't Really See Us Eradicating It,'" *The Hill* (Washington, DC), July 22, 2020. https://thehill.com.

38. Quoted in Robin Foster and E.J. Mundell, "Antibody Study Suggests More Lasting Immunity Against COVID than Believed," *U.S. News & World Report*, September 2, 2020. www.usnews.com.

39. Quoted in Michael Le Page, "Is Sweden's Coronavirus Strategy a Cautionary Tale or a Success Story?," *New Scientist*, August 13, 2020. www.newscientist.com.

40. Quoted in Akshay Syal, "COVID-19 Antibodies May Last for at Least 4 Months, Icelandic Study Suggests," NBC News, September 1, 2020. www.nbcnews.com.

41. Quoted in Will Feuer, "U.S. Agrees to Pay Pfizer and BioNTech $2 Billion for 100 Million Doses of Coronavirus Vaccine," CNBC, July 22, 2020. www.cnbc.com.

42. Quoted in Talha Khan Burki, "The Russian Vaccine for COVID-19," *The Lancet*, September 4, 2020. www.thelancet.com.

43. Quoted in Burki, "The Russian Vaccine for COVID-19."

44. Quoted in US Food and Drug Administration, "FDA in Brief: FDA Issues Guidance on Emergency Use Authorization for COVID-19 Vaccines," October 6, 2020. www.fda.gov.

45. Quoted in Berkeley Lovelace Jr. and Noah Higgins-Dunn, "Dr. Anthony Fauci Says Chance of Coronavirus Vaccine Being Highly Effective Is 'Not Great,'" CNBC, August 7, 2020. www.cnbc.com.

46. Quoted in Lovelace and Higgins-Dunn, "Dr. Anthony Fauci Says Chance of Coronavirus Vaccine Being Highly Effective Is 'Not Great.'"

47. Quoted in Hellmann, "Fauci on Coronavirus."

### Centers for Disease Control and Prevention (CDC)

www.cdc.gov/coronavirus/2019-ncov

The CDC is the nation's premier public health protection agency. The agency's website devotes significant space to coronavirus and COVID-19 facts and statistics. The site also has extensive information on who is at risk, protective measures, contact tracing, community response, schools and youth, and more.

### Johns Hopkins Coronavirus Resource Center (CRC)

https://coronavirus.jhu.edu

The CRC, created and run by Johns Hopkins University & Medicine, is a continuously updated source of COVID-19 data and expert guidance. The center gathers and analyzes statistics and other information related to COVID-19 cases, testing, contact tracing, and vaccine research. The site also provides links to numerous articles from a variety of sources.

### National Institute of Allergy and Infectious Diseases (NIAID)

www.niaid.nih.gov

The NIAID is one of the twenty-seven institutes and centers that make up the National Institutes of Health. Its website includes information about coronaviruses, the public health and government response to COVID-19, and treatment guidelines. It also provides details on volunteering for prevention clinical studies.

### National Institutes of Health (NIH)

www.nih.gov/coronavirus

Part of the US Department of Health and Human Services, the NIH is the largest biomedical research agency in the world. Its website provides information on development of COVID-19 vaccines, testing, and treatments as well as links to other related topics.

## US Food & Drug Administration (FDA)

www.fda.gov

The FDA regulates drugs, medical devices, and other products and oversees food safety. Its website provides pandemic-related statistics and information on protective equipment, treatments, and testing. It includes an extensive section of frequently asked questions about a variety of COVID-19 topics.

## World Health Organization (WHO)

www.who.int/emergencies/diseases/novel-coronavirus-2019

Working within the framework of the United Nations, the WHO directs and coordinates global health issues. Its website features rolling coronavirus updates, situation reports, travel advice, facts about preventive measures such as masks, information on how the virus spreads, and more.

**Additional resources:** City, county, and state public health departments

## Books

Steven R. Feldman and Veronica K. Emmerich, *Will It Ever Go Away? Practical Answers to Your Questions About COVID-19*. Rand-Smith, 2020.

Richard Horton, *The COVID-19 Catastrophe: What's Gone Wrong and How to Stop It Happening Again*. Cambridge, UK: Polity Press, 2020.

Debora MacKenzie, *COVID-19: The Pandemic That Never Should Have Happened and How to Stop the Next One*. New York: Hachette, 2020.

Hal Marcovitz, *The COVID-19 Pandemic: The World Turned Upside Down*. San Diego, CA: ReferencePoint, 2021.

Michael Mosley, *COVID-19: Everything You Need to Know About the Corona Virus and the Race for the Vaccine*. New York: Atria, 2020.

Klaus Schwab and Thierry Malleret, *COVID-19: The Great Reset*. Zurich, Switzerland: ISBN Agentur Schweiz, 2020.

## Internet Sources

Paul Biasco, "All the Things George W. Bush Said We Should Do to Prepare for a Pandemic That Donald Trump Ignored," *Business Insider*, May 31, 2020. www.businessinsider.com.

Nicholas Christakis, "Responding to Covid-19," *The Economist*, August 10, 2020. www.economist.com.

Pien Huang et al., "Essential Vocab for COVID-19: From Asymptomatic to Zoonotic," NPR, June 27, 2020. www.npr.org.

Johns Hopkins University & Medicine, "COVID-19 in the USA," September 25, 2020. https://coronavirus.jhu.edu.

Emily Oster and Galit Alter, "Immunity from COVID," COVID Explained, August 26, 2020. www.explaincovid.org.

*Washington Post*, "At Least 204,000 People Have Died from Coronavirus in the U.S.," September 26, 2020. www.washingtonpost.com.

Ed Yong, "Why the Coronavirus Has Been So Successful," *The Atlantic*, March 20, 2020. www.theatlantic.com.